Table Of Contents

Understanding Private Placements 3
Benefits of Investing in Private Placements 3
Risks Associated with Private Placements 3
Regulations and Legal Considerations for Private Placements 3
Chapter 2: Investing in Private Placements for Real Estate.................3
Overview of Real Estate Private Placements 3
Evaluating Real Estate Investment Opportunities 3
Due Diligence for Real Estate Private Placements...........................3
Investing Strategies for Real Estate Private Placements................3
Chapter 3: Investing in Private Placements for Startups 3
Introduction to Startup Private Placements.....................................3
Assessing Startup Investment Opportunities 3
Conducting Due Diligence for Startup Private Placements...........3
Investment Strategies for Startup Private Placements 3
Chapter 4: Investing in Private Placements for Biotech Companies..3
Overview of Biotech Private Placements 3
Analyzing Biotech Investment Opportunities 3
Due Diligence for Biotech Private Placements.................................3
Investment Strategies for Biotech Private Placements...................3
Chapter 5: Investing in Private Placements for Renewable Energy
Projects 3
Introduction to Renewable Energy Private Placements.................3
Evaluating Renewable Energy Investment Opportunities 3
Due Diligence for Renewable Energy Private Placements..............3
Investment Strategies for Renewable Energy Private Placements3
Chapter 6: Investing in Private Placements for Art and Collectibles..3

Overview of Art and Collectibles Private Placements 3
Assessing Art and Collectibles Investment Opportunities..............3
Conducting Due Diligence for Art and Collectibles Private
Placements..3
Investment Strategies for Art and Collectibles Private Placements
....3

Chapter 7: Investing in Private Placements for Technology
Companies..3
Introduction to Technology Private Placements.............................3
Analyzing Technology Investment Opportunities..........................3
Due Diligence for Technology Private Placements.........................3
Investment Strategies for Technology Private Placements............3
Chapter 8: Investing in Private Placements for Healthcare Startups.3
Overview of Healthcare Private Placements 3
Evaluating Healthcare Investment Opportunities 3
Due Diligence for Healthcare Private Placements..........................3
Investment Strategies for Healthcare Private Placements............3
Chapter 9: Investing in Private Placements for Food and Beverage
Businesses..3
Introduction to Food and Beverage Private Placements................3
Assessing Food and Beverage Investment Opportunities..............3
Conducting Due Diligence for Food and Beverage Private
Placements 3
Investment Strategies for Food and Beverage Private Placements
....3

Chapter 10: Investing in Private Placements for Social Impact
Projects 3
Overview of Social Impact Private Placements 3
Analyzing Social Impact Investment Opportunities 3
Due Diligence for Social Impact Private Placements......................3
Investment Strategies for Social Impact Private Placements.........3
Chapter 11: Investing in Private Placements for Entertainment and
Media Ventures...3
Introduction to Entertainment and Media Private Placements.....3
Evaluating Entertainment and Media Investment Opportunities .3
Due Diligence for Entertainment and Media Private Placements .3

Investment Strategies for Entertainment and Media Private
Placements 3
Chapter 12: Conclusion..3
Recap of Private Placements Investing Strategies.........................3
Chapter 1: Introduction to Private Placements 1

Appendices

1. Stock Exchanges around the World

2. How to participate in the Toronto Venture Exchange

3. Where to find Private Placement Investment Opportunities

Chapter 1: Introduction to Private Placements

Understanding Private Placements

Private placements have emerged as an exclusive investment opportunity for savvy investors looking to diversify their portfolios and gain access to high potential returns. In this subchapter, we will delve into the intricacies of private placements and explore various niches such as real estate, startups, biotech companies, renewable energy projects, art and collectibles, technology companies, healthcare startups, food and beverage businesses, social impact projects, and entertainment and media ventures.

Private placements refer to the sale of securities to a select group of investors, typically institutions, high net worth individuals, or accredited investors. Unlike public offerings, private placements are not registered with the Securities and Exchange Commission (SEC) and are subject to certain exemptions under the securities laws. This exclusivity allows investors to participate in unique investment opportunities that may not be available through traditional channels. Investing in private placements requires a thorough understanding of the niche market and the specific risks associated with each industry. For instance, investing in private placements for real estate offers the potential for substantial returns, but investors must carefully analyze market trends, location, and the expertise of the project developers. Similarly, investing in private placements for startups involves evaluating the business model, management team, competitive landscape, and potential for scalability.

Private placements for biotech companies can be highly lucrative, but investors must consider the inherent risks associated with drug development, clinical trials, and regulatory approval. Renewable energy projects offer investors a chance to support sustainable initiatives while reaping financial rewards, but due diligence is crucial to assess the project's viability, technology, and government policies.

Investing in private placements for art and collectibles allows investors to diversify their portfolios beyond traditional assets, but understanding the art market, provenance, and valuation is essential. Technology companies, healthcare startups, food and beverage businesses, social impact projects, and entertainment and media ventures each have their own unique dynamics, requiring investors to carefully evaluate market potential, competitive advantages, and growth prospects.

While private placements offer exclusive investment opportunities, it is important to note that they are generally illiquid and may have limited exit strategies. Investors should conduct thorough due diligence, seek professional advice, and carefully consider their risk tolerance and investment objectives before participating in private placements.

In conclusion, understanding private placements is essential for investors seeking to explore exclusive investment opportunities in various niches. By comprehending the specific risks and opportunities associated with each industry, investors can make informed investment decisions and potentially benefit from high potential returns. However, it is crucial to approach private placements with caution, conduct thorough due diligence, and seek professional guidance to mitigate risks and maximize the chances of success.

Benefits of Investing in Private Placements

Private placements offer a unique and exclusive investment opportunity that can provide significant benefits to investors across various industries and niches. Whether you are interested in real estate, startups, biotech companies, renewable energy projects, art and collectibles, technology companies, healthcare startups, food and beverage businesses, social impact projects, or entertainment and media ventures, investing in private placements can be a fruitful endeavor. In this subchapter, we will explore the key benefits of investing in private placements and how they can help diversify your portfolio and generate higher returns.

1. Access to Exclusive Opportunities: Private placements provide investors with access to investment opportunities that are not available to the general public. This exclusivity allows investors to tap into promising ventures and industries that have the potential for significant growth and profitability.

2. Potential for Higher Returns: Private placements often offer higher returns compared to traditional investment options. By investing in companies at an early stage or projects with high growth potential, investors can benefit from the appreciation of their investment over time.

3. Diversification: Private placements enable investors to diversify their portfolios by investing in different industries and niches. This diversification helps mitigate risk and can lead to more stable and consistent returns.

4. Active Involvement: Investing in private placements allows investors to have a more active role in the success of the venture. Unlike public investments, private placements often provide opportunities for investors to contribute their expertise and guidance, which can enhance the chances of success and increase investor satisfaction.

5. Tax Advantages: Private placements can offer significant tax advantages, such as tax deductions, deferrals, or exemptions. These benefits can help investors optimize their tax liabilities and potentially increase their overall investment returns.

6. Potential for Early Liquidity: While private placements are typically illiquid investments, they can provide the potential for early

liquidity. This means that investors may have the opportunity to exit their investment earlier than expected, allowing them to realize their returns sooner.

7. Social Impact: Investing in private placements focused on social impact projects allows investors to make a positive difference in the world while also generating financial returns. This aligns with the growing trend of impact investing, where investors seek to create social and environmental change through their investment choices.

In conclusion, investing in private placements offers a range of benefits to investors across various niches. From the potential for higher returns and tax advantages to the opportunity for active involvement and social impact, private placements provide a unique avenue for diversification and growth. By understanding the specific benefits associated with investing in private placements in your chosen niche, you can make informed investment decisions and unlock the potential for significant financial gains.

Risks Associated with Private Placements

Private placements offer investors exclusive investment opportunities that are not available through traditional public markets. While these investments can offer attractive returns, it is important for investors to understand and carefully consider the risks associated with private placements before making any investment decisions.

1. Lack of liquidity: One of the main risks with private placements is the lack of liquidity. Unlike publicly traded securities, private placements are generally not easily bought or sold on a secondary market. Investors may have to hold onto their investment for an

extended period of time, and it may be difficult to access their capital before the investment matures or an exit opportunity arises.

2. High risk: Private placements are often considered high-risk investments. Startups, biotech companies, renewable energy projects, and other ventures in the private placement space may have a higher failure rate compared to more established companies. Investors should be aware that they could lose their entire investment if the company or project fails.

3. Limited information: Private placements usually provide limited information compared to publicly traded companies. Investors may not have access to the same level of financial disclosures, audited statements, or regulatory oversight. It is crucial for investors to conduct thorough due diligence and understand the risks associated with the specific investment opportunity.

4. Lack of transparency: Private placements are typically not subject to the same level of regulatory oversight as public offerings. This lack of transparency can make it difficult for investors to fully evaluate the investment and assess the company's financial health, management team, or potential risks. Investors should carefully review the offering documents and seek professional advice if needed.

5. Valuation challenges: Valuing private placements can be challenging due to the limited market data and lack of transparency. Determining the fair value of the investment can be subjective and may be influenced by factors such as the stage of the company, industry trends, and market conditions. Investors should be cautious and understand the potential risks associated with valuation uncertainty.

6. Lack of diversification: Private placements often require a significant investment amount, which can limit an investor's ability to diversify their portfolio. Concentrating investments in a single

private placement exposes investors to higher risk if the investment does not perform as expected.

In conclusion, while private placements can offer unique investment opportunities, they come with inherent risks. Investors should carefully evaluate the risks associated with each private placement opportunity and consider their risk tolerance, investment objectives, and the potential impact on their overall investment portfolio. Seeking the advice of a qualified financial advisor can also help investors navigate the complexities and mitigate the risks associated with private placements.

Regulations and Legal Considerations for Private Placements

Private placements offer investors the opportunity to participate in exclusive investment opportunities that are not available to the general public. However, engaging in private placements requires a thorough understanding of the regulations and legal considerations that govern these investments. This subchapter will provide valuable insights and guidance on navigating the regulatory landscape of private placements, ensuring that investors can make informed decisions and mitigate potential risks.

Regulatory Framework

Private placements are subject to various regulations imposed by regulatory bodies such as the Securities and Exchange Commission (SEC) in the United States. These regulations aim to protect investors by ensuring transparency, disclosure, and fair practices in the private placement market. It is essential for investors to familiarize themselves with the specific regulatory requirements in their jurisdiction to ensure compliance.

Accredited Investor Status

One key requirement for participating in private placements is having accredited investor status. Accredited investors are individuals or entities that meet certain income or net worth thresholds, demonstrating their ability to bear the risks associated with private placements. Understanding the criteria for accredited investor status is crucial for investors looking to access exclusive investment opportunities.

Disclosure Requirements

Private placements are subject to strict disclosure requirements to ensure that investors have access to all material information necessary to make informed investment decisions. This includes detailed information about the issuing company, its financials, risks involved, and potential returns. Investors should carefully review all disclosure documents provided by the issuer before making any investment commitments.

Legal Considerations

Investing in private placements also involves various legal considerations. Investors should carefully review and understand the terms and conditions of the investment, including rights, restrictions, and potential exit strategies. It is advisable to consult with legal professionals experienced in private placements to ensure that the investment aligns with the investor's goals and objectives.

Risk Mitigation

Private placements inherently involve higher risks compared to traditional investments. Therefore, it is crucial for investors to conduct thorough due diligence on the issuing company, its management team, and the specific investment opportunity. Engaging professional advisors, such as accountants and lawyers, can provide valuable insights and help identify potential risks.

Conclusion

Understanding the regulations and legal considerations for private placements is essential for investors seeking exclusive investment opportunities. By familiarizing themselves with the regulatory framework, accreditation requirements, disclosure obligations, and legal considerations, investors can make informed decisions and mitigate potential risks. Engaging professional advice and conducting thorough due diligence are key to successful private placement investments. This subchapter aims to equip investors with the necessary knowledge and tools to navigate the regulatory landscape and make sound investment decisions across various niches, including real estate, startups, biotech companies, renewable energy projects, art and collectibles, technology companies, healthcare startups, food and beverage businesses, social impact projects, and entertainment and media ventures.

Chapter 2: Investing in Private Placements for Real Estate

Overview of Real Estate Private Placements

Real estate private placements offer investors a unique opportunity to participate in exclusive real estate projects that may not be available through traditional investment channels. This subchapter will provide an overview of real estate private placements, discussing what they are, how they work, and the benefits they offer to investors.

A real estate private placement is a type of investment offering that allows individuals to invest directly in real estate projects. These projects can range from residential and commercial properties to development projects and other real estate ventures. Unlike public investments, private placements are typically not registered with regulatory authorities, which means they are only available to a select group of investors.

One of the main advantages of investing in real estate private placements is the potential for higher returns. These investments often come with a higher level of risk, but they can also offer significant rewards. Real estate has historically been a lucrative investment, and private placements provide a way for investors to access exclusive opportunities that have the potential for even greater returns.

Another benefit of real estate private placements is the ability to diversify one's investment portfolio. By investing in different types of real estate projects, investors can spread their risk and potentially increase their overall returns. This diversification can be especially valuable for individuals who are looking to invest in specific niches, such as renewable energy projects, art and collectibles, or healthcare startups.

Investing in real estate private placements also provides investors with a level of control and transparency that may not be available in other investment options. Unlike publicly traded real estate investment trusts (REITs), private placements allow investors to have a direct say in the management and decision-making of the project. This level of involvement can provide a sense of security and satisfaction for investors who want to have a hands-on approach to their investments.

In summary, real estate private placements offer investors a unique opportunity to invest in exclusive real estate projects that may not be available through traditional investment channels. These investments provide the potential for higher returns, diversification, and greater control over one's investment portfolio. Whether you are interested in investing in real estate for renewable energy projects, technology companies, or social impact projects, real estate private placements can be a valuable addition to your investment strategy.

Evaluating Real Estate Investment Opportunities

When it comes to investing in real estate, it is crucial to thoroughly evaluate the investment opportunities available to ensure you make informed decisions. This subchapter aims to guide investors in evaluating real estate investment opportunities, equipping them with the necessary knowledge and expertise to invest wisely in this lucrative market.

Firstly, it is essential to conduct thorough due diligence on the property being considered for investment. This includes analyzing the location, market trends, and economic indicators. Understanding the local real estate market and its potential for growth is key to identifying profitable opportunities.

Investors should also assess the property's financials, including the potential return on investment (ROI). This involves evaluating rental income potential, property expenses, and any additional costs associated with the investment. Conducting a detailed financial analysis will help determine if the investment aligns with your financial goals and risk tolerance.

Furthermore, it is crucial to evaluate the reputation and track record of the real estate developer or management team responsible for the investment opportunity. Research their past projects, success rates, and overall experience in the industry. A reputable and experienced team increases the likelihood of a successful investment.

Diversification is another essential aspect to consider when evaluating real estate investment opportunities. Diversifying your portfolio across different types of properties, such as residential, commercial, or industrial, helps mitigate risks and maximize returns. It is also advisable to diversify across different geographic locations to reduce exposure to regional market fluctuations.

Lastly, investors should carefully review the legal and regulatory aspects of the investment opportunity. This includes examining the terms and conditions of the private placement, understanding the rights and responsibilities of the investor, and seeking professional advice if necessary. Being well-informed about the legal framework ensures compliance and protection of your investment.

In conclusion, evaluating real estate investment opportunities requires a systematic approach that considers factors such as location, financial analysis, reputation of the management team, diversification, and legal aspects. By following this comprehensive evaluation process, investors can make informed decisions that align with their financial goals and risk tolerance.

Due Diligence for Real Estate Private Placements

Investing in private placements can offer investors exclusive opportunities to diversify their portfolios and potentially earn higher returns. Real estate private placements, in particular, have gained popularity due to their potential for steady income and long-term capital appreciation. However, before diving into these investments, it is crucial for investors to conduct due diligence to mitigate risks and make informed decisions.

When investing in real estate private placements, investors should begin by thoroughly researching the issuer or sponsor of the project. This includes examining the sponsor's track record, experience, and reputation in the industry. Investors should consider the sponsor's past performance in similar projects, their financial stability, and their ability to manage the investment effectively.

Furthermore, investors should analyze the specific real estate project being offered through the private placement. This entails reviewing the property's location, market conditions, and potential for growth. Investors should assess the property's income potential, occupancy rates, and any potential legal or environmental risks associated with it.

In addition to evaluating the sponsor and the property, investors should carefully review the private placement memorandum (PPM), which provides detailed information about the investment opportunity. The PPM should outline the investment's objectives, risks, and terms, including the expected return on investment and the duration of the project. Investors should also pay attention to the offering structure, fees, and any conflicts of interest disclosed in the PPM.

Furthermore, investors should seek professional advice from attorneys, accountants, or financial advisors who specialize in real estate investments. These professionals can help investors navigate the complexities of private placements and provide valuable insights into the potential risks and rewards.

Lastly, investors should consider their own investment objectives, risk tolerance, and time horizon before committing to a real estate private placement. It is crucial to align the investment opportunity with one's personal financial goals and to ensure that the investment fits within their overall portfolio strategy.

In conclusion, conducting due diligence is essential when investing in real estate private placements. By thoroughly researching the sponsor, analyzing the property, reviewing the PPM, seeking professional advice, and aligning the investment with personal goals, investors can make informed decisions and increase their chances of success in this exclusive investment niche.

Investing Strategies for Real Estate Private Placements

Real estate private placements offer investors the opportunity to participate in exclusive opportunities within the real estate market. These investments can provide attractive returns and diversification to an investment portfolio. However, investing in real estate private placements requires careful consideration and the implementation of effective strategies. In this subchapter, we will explore some key investment strategies for real estate private placements.

1. Research and Due Diligence: Before investing in any real estate private placement, it is crucial to conduct thorough research and due diligence. This includes analyzing the track record and reputation of the sponsor or developer, assessing the underlying real estate assets, and evaluating the potential risks and returns. Investors should also review the legal documentation and financials of the investment opportunity.

2. Diversification: Diversification is a fundamental strategy for any investment portfolio, including real estate private placements. By diversifying across different types of properties, locations, and sponsors, investors can reduce their exposure to specific risks and increase their chances of achieving positive returns. It is important to carefully analyze the correlation and risk factors of each investment to ensure true diversification.

3. Aligning Investment Goals: When investing in real estate private placements, it is essential to align the investment goals with the specific opportunity. Different private placements may focus on various real estate sectors such as residential, commercial, industrial, or mixed-use properties. Investors should consider their risk tolerance, investment horizon, and return objectives to ensure the investment aligns with their overall wealth-building strategy.

4. Professional Management: Real estate private placements often involve active management by experienced professionals. It is important to assess the expertise and track record of the management team responsible for overseeing the investment. A team with a proven ability to execute the investment strategy, handle property management, and navigate market cycles can significantly enhance the chances of success.

5. Exit Strategy: Before investing in a real estate private placement, investors should carefully consider the exit strategy. Some investments may have a specific timeline, such as a development project with a target completion date, while others may have a longer holding period. Understanding the exit strategy and potential liquidity options is crucial to ensure the investment aligns with the investor's financial goals and timeline.

In conclusion, investing in real estate private placements can offer unique opportunities for investors seeking exposure to the real estate market. By implementing effective strategies such as thorough research, diversification, aligning investment goals, professional management, and considering exit strategies, investors can increase their chances of achieving attractive returns and mitigating risks in this exclusive investment niche.

Chapter 3: Investing in Private Placements for Startups

Introduction to Startup Private Placements

Private placements can be an excellent way for investors to access exclusive investment opportunities and potentially generate significant returns. This subchapter will provide an introductory overview of startup private placements, highlighting the benefits, risks, and considerations associated with investing in this niche. Startup private placements offer investors the chance to invest in early-stage companies that are not yet publicly traded. These companies are often at a critical stage of their development, seeking capital to fund growth, research and development, or product commercialization. By investing in a startup private placement, investors can become early stakeholders in these companies and potentially benefit from their future success.

One key advantage of investing in startup private placements is the potential for high returns. As startups often have exponential growth potential, successful investments can yield significant profits. However, it's important to note that these investments also carry a higher level of risk compared to more established companies. Startups are inherently more vulnerable to failure, and there is a greater likelihood of losing the entire investment.

Investing in startup private placements requires careful consideration and due diligence. Investors should thoroughly research and understand the industry, market potential, competitive landscape, and management team of the startup. Conducting a thorough analysis of the business model, financial projections, and intellectual property can help investors make informed investment decisions.

It's also crucial to evaluate the terms of the private placement offering. This includes understanding the investment amount required, the valuation of the company, the equity or debt structure, and any potential dilution risks. Investors should assess the liquidity options available and the potential exit strategies, such as initial public offerings (IPOs), mergers, or acquisitions.

Startup private placements exist across various sectors, catering to different investor interests. Whether it's real estate, biotech, renewable energy, art, technology, healthcare, food and beverage, social impact, or entertainment and media ventures, there are specialized private placements available. Each sector has its unique considerations and investment opportunities, making it essential for investors to understand the specificities of each niche.

In conclusion, startup private placements offer investors the opportunity to invest in early-stage companies with high growth potential. While these investments come with higher risks, they can also yield substantial returns. Thorough research, due diligence, and understanding of the terms and industry specifics are vital for successful investments. With the availability of private placements in various sectors, investors can explore niche opportunities that align with their interests and investment goals.

Assessing Startup Investment Opportunities

Investing in startup companies can be an exciting and potentially lucrative venture for investors looking to diversify their portfolios and support innovative ideas. However, it is crucial to approach these opportunities with caution and conduct thorough assessments before committing your capital. In this subchapter, we will explore the key factors to consider when assessing startup investment opportunities across various niches, including real estate, biotech, renewable energy, art and collectibles, technology, healthcare, food and beverage, social impact projects, and entertainment and media ventures.

Firstly, it is essential to evaluate the startup's business model and market potential. Understand the industry landscape and identify the startup's unique value proposition. Assess the demand for their product or service and analyze the competitive environment. Look for startups that offer innovative solutions to existing problems, as these have higher growth potential.

Next, scrutinize the startup's management team. A strong and experienced team is crucial for success. Evaluate their track record, industry expertise, and ability to execute the business plan effectively. Assess their passion, commitment, and ability to adapt to market changes.

Financial due diligence is another critical aspect of assessing startup investment opportunities. Review the startup's financial projections, revenue streams, and cost structure. Evaluate their funding needs and understand how the investment will be utilized. Assess the startup's valuation and compare it to industry benchmarks to determine its attractiveness.

Furthermore, consider the startup's legal and regulatory environment. Assess any potential legal risks, such as intellectual property disputes or regulatory hurdles. Understand the startup's compliance with applicable laws and regulations.

Additionally, consider the startup's scalability and exit strategy. Evaluate the potential for growth and expansion, as well as the likelihood of attracting future rounds of funding. Assess the startup's exit options, such as an initial public offering (IPO) or acquisition, and the potential returns for investors.

Lastly, it is vital to conduct thorough research and seek expert advice. Engage with industry professionals, attend startup pitch events, and network with other investors. Leverage due diligence platforms and seek guidance from investment advisors or venture capitalists with experience in the niche you are interested in. Investing in startup companies can be highly rewarding, but it also carries inherent risks. By carefully assessing startup investment opportunities based on their business model, management team, financials, legal environment, scalability, and exit strategy, investors can make informed decisions and increase their chances of success in this exciting asset class.

Conducting Due Diligence for Startup Private Placements

When it comes to investing in private placements, particularly those in the startup ecosystem, conducting thorough due diligence is essential. As an investor, it is crucial to ensure that you are making informed decisions and mitigating potential risks. This chapter will guide you through the process of conducting due diligence for startup private placements, providing you with actionable steps to make sound investment choices.

1. Understanding the Startup Landscape: Before diving into due diligence, it is imperative to have a clear understanding of the startup landscape and the specific industry you are considering investing in. This knowledge will help you identify potential opportunities and assess the viability of the startup's business model.

2. Assessing the Management Team: The success of any startup heavily relies on its management team. Evaluate the team's experience, track record, and expertise in the industry. Look for strong leadership, complementary skill sets, and a proven ability to execute on the business plan.

3. Evaluating the Business Model: Scrutinize the startup's business model to understand its revenue streams, market potential, and

competitive advantage. Assess the scalability and sustainability of the business, and consider the potential risks and challenges it may face.

4. Analyzing Financials: Thoroughly review the startup's financial statements, including revenue, expenses, and projected growth. Evaluate the company's burn rate, cash flow, and potential funding needs. Assess the company's valuation and compare it to industry benchmarks to determine if it is reasonable.

5. Assessing Intellectual Property: For technology startups, intellectual property (IP) is often a crucial asset. Confirm the ownership and protection of any patents, trademarks, or copyrights held by the company. Evaluate the strength and uniqueness of the IP portfolio and assess its potential for generating revenue.

6. Examining Legal and Regulatory Compliance: Ensure that the startup is compliant with all relevant laws and regulations. Review any legal agreements, contracts, permits, or licenses that the company holds. Consider the potential risks associated with regulatory changes or legal disputes.

7. Conducting Background Checks: Perform thorough background checks on the startup's founders, management team, and key stakeholders. Look for any red flags, such as previous bankruptcies, legal issues, or conflicts of interest. Assess the team's reputation and integrity.

8. Seeking Professional Advice: Consider engaging professionals, such as attorneys, accountants, or industry experts, to assist with due diligence. Their expertise can provide valuable insights and help you navigate complex investment opportunities.

Remember, conducting due diligence is an ongoing process. Stay updated on the startup's progress, market conditions, and any relevant industry news. Regularly reassess your investment thesis and make adjustments as necessary. By conducting thorough due diligence, you can increase your chances of making successful investments in startup private placements across various niches, including real estate, biotech, renewable energy, technology, healthcare, and more.

Investment Strategies for Startup Private Placements

Investing in startup private placements can be an exciting and potentially lucrative opportunity for investors looking to diversify their portfolios and support innovative new businesses. However, it is important to approach these investments with caution and develop a well-thought-out investment strategy. In this subchapter, we will explore some effective investment strategies for investing in startup private placements across various niches, including real estate, biotech, renewable energy, art, technology, healthcare, food and beverage, social impact projects, and entertainment and media ventures.

1. Conduct Thorough Due Diligence: Before investing in any startup private placement, it is crucial to conduct thorough due diligence. This includes researching the company's management team, financials, market potential, competitive landscape, and growth prospects. Additionally, investors should carefully review the offering memorandum and seek advice from professionals, such as attorneys and financial advisors, to ensure they fully understand the risks and potential rewards of the investment.

2. Diversify Your Portfolio: Investing in startup private placements involves a higher level of risk compared to traditional investments. To mitigate this risk, investors should consider diversifying their portfolio by investing in multiple startups across different niches. This helps spread the risk and increases the chances of achieving positive returns.

3. Seek Industry-Specific Opportunities: Different industries have unique investment characteristics and risk profiles. By focusing on specific niches, such as real estate, biotech, renewable energy, art, technology, healthcare, food and beverage, social impact projects, or entertainment and media ventures, investors can develop a deeper understanding of the industry dynamics and identify potentially lucrative investment opportunities.

4. Consider Co-Investing or Joining Syndicates: Investing alongside experienced investors or joining syndicates can provide valuable insights, expertise, and access to a broader network. Co-investing or participating in syndicates can also help mitigate risks and increase the chances of successful investments.

5. Assess the Exit Strategy: Startup private placements typically involve a longer investment horizon compared to publicly traded stocks. Therefore, it is essential to assess the exit strategy before investing. This includes understanding the company's plans for an initial public offering (IPO), merger, acquisition, or other liquidity events that may allow investors to realize their returns.

In conclusion, investing in startup private placements can offer investors exciting opportunities to support innovative businesses in various industries. However, it is crucial to develop a sound investment strategy, conduct thorough due diligence, diversify the portfolio, focus on niche industries, consider co-investing or joining syndicates, and assess the exit strategy. By following these investment strategies, investors can increase their chances of success in the dynamic world of startup private placements.

process of analyzing biotech investment opportunities, including key factors to consider and potential risks involved.

When evaluating biotech companies for investment, investors should begin by assessing the company's technology and intellectual property portfolio. Biotech companies heavily rely on their technological advancements and proprietary assets, such as patents and licenses, to drive value and maintain a competitive edge. Investors should examine the novelty and potential of the company's technology, ensuring it addresses significant unmet needs in the market.

Another crucial aspect to consider is the biotech company's pipeline of products or therapies. Investors should evaluate the stage of development for each product, as well as the clinical trial results and regulatory progress. It is essential to understand the market potential and the competitive landscape for each product, as well as any risks or challenges that may impact commercialization.

Financial analysis is also critical when analyzing biotech investment opportunities. Investors should review the company's financial statements, including revenue and expense projections, cash flow analysis, and balance sheet strength. Assessing the company's ability to secure additional funding, whether through private placements or other means, is vital to ensure continued operations and development.

Furthermore, investors should evaluate the management team's experience and track record in the biotech industry. The success of a biotech company often hinges on the expertise and vision of its leadership. Investors should consider the management team's ability to execute on their strategic plans and navigate the complexities of the biotech sector.

While biotech investments offer significant growth potential, it is crucial to acknowledge the inherent risks associated with this sector. Factors such as regulatory hurdles, clinical trial failures, and intellectual property disputes can significantly impact the value and viability of a biotech investment. Investors must carefully assess these risks and develop risk mitigation strategies to protect their capital.

In conclusion, analyzing biotech investment opportunities requires a comprehensive evaluation of technological advancements, intellectual property, product pipeline, financials, management team, and risk factors. By conducting thorough due diligence, investors can make informed decisions and identify biotech investments with the potential for substantial returns. However, it is important to remember that investing in the biotech sector involves inherent risks, and investors should consult with their financial advisors before making any investment decisions.

Due Diligence for Biotech Private Placements

When it comes to investing in biotech private placements, conducting thorough due diligence is crucial. This subchapter will guide investors through the process of evaluating biotech investment opportunities and making informed decisions.

Biotech companies operate in a highly specialized and complex industry, with unique risks and potential for high returns. To navigate this landscape effectively, investors must delve into the following key aspects during due diligence:

1. Technology and Intellectual Property: Understanding the core technology and intellectual property of a biotech company is essential. Evaluate patents, licenses, and any potential legal issues that may impact the company's ability to commercialize its products.

2. Management Team: Assess the experience, expertise, and track record of the management team. Biotech companies rely heavily on

scientific knowledge and regulatory expertise, so having a capable team is critical for success.

3. Product Pipeline: Analyze the company's product pipeline and assess the potential market size, competitive landscape, and regulatory hurdles. Look for a diversified portfolio of products at various stages of development to mitigate risk.

4. Clinical Trials: Investigate the results and progress of any ongoing or completed clinical trials. Understand the trial design, patient population, and potential risks and benefits. Seek independent expert opinions to evaluate the trial's validity.

5. Regulatory Environment: Biotech investments are subject to stringent regulatory oversight. Familiarize yourself with the relevant regulatory bodies and their requirements. Assess the company's compliance history and any potential regulatory challenges it may face.

6. Financials and Funding: Review the company's financial statements, funding history, and burn rate. Biotech companies often require significant capital to fund research and development. Evaluate the company's financial stability and its ability to secure further funding.

7. Market Opportunity: Understand the market potential for the company's products and estimate the potential return on investment. Consider factors such as market size, competitive advantages, and barriers to entry.

8. Exit Strategy: Assess the potential exit options for your investment. Biotech companies may seek to go public, be acquired, or license their products. Evaluate the feasibility and potential returns of each exit strategy.

Remember, investing in biotech private placements carries inherent risks, including the potential for product failures, regulatory setbacks, and market volatility. Engage with experts in the biotech industry, such as consultants, analysts, or advisors, to gain deeper insights and mitigate risks.

By conducting thorough due diligence on biotech private placements, investors can make more informed investment decisions and increase their chances of achieving profitable returns in this exciting and rapidly evolving sector.

Investment Strategies for Biotech Private Placements

Investing in biotech private placements can be an exciting and potentially lucrative opportunity for investors looking to capitalize on the advancements in the biotechnology industry. However, it is essential to understand the unique challenges and risks associated with investing in this niche. This subchapter will provide you with valuable insights and strategies to navigate the world of biotech private placements effectively.

1. Do Your Due Diligence: Before investing in any biotech private placement, thoroughly research the company and its management team. Evaluate their track record, expertise, and previous successes in the industry. Look for companies with a solid pipeline of products, strong intellectual property portfolio, and partnerships with reputable organizations.

2. Understand the Science: Biotech investments are inherently complex due to the scientific nature of the industry. Take the time to understand the underlying science behind the company's products or therapies. Consider consulting with experts or engaging with industry professionals to gain a deeper understanding of the technology and its potential market impact.

3. Diversify Your Portfolio: Biotech investments can be highly volatile and carry significant risks. To mitigate these risks, diversify

your portfolio by investing in multiple biotech companies with varying stages of development, therapeutic areas, and technologies. This strategy will help spread out your risk and increase the chances of finding a successful investment.

4. Stay Updated on Regulatory Environment: The biotech industry is heavily regulated, and changes in regulations can have a significant impact on companies' prospects. Stay updated on regulatory developments, such as FDA approvals and clinical trial results. Be aware of the potential risks associated with regulatory hurdles and factor them into your investment decisions.

5. Partner with Experts: Consider partnering with experienced biotech investors or venture capital firms specializing in the industry. They often have a deep understanding of the sector, access to exclusive investment opportunities, and the expertise to evaluate potential risks and returns. Collaborating with such experts can enhance your chances of making successful biotech investments.

6. Long-term Horizon: Biotech investments often require a long-term perspective. Many companies in this sector take years to develop and commercialize their products. Be prepared for potential delays in the clinical trial process and regulatory approvals. Patience and a long-term investment horizon are crucial for success in the biotech space.

Remember, investing in biotech private placements involves substantial risks, including the potential for loss of capital. It is crucial to consult with financial advisors and conduct thorough research before making any investment decisions. By applying these investment strategies and staying informed about the biotech industry, you can increase your chances of finding promising investment opportunities in this exciting and rapidly evolving field.

Chapter 5: Investing in Private Placements for Renewable Energy Projects

Introduction to Renewable Energy Private Placements

Renewable energy has become an increasingly attractive investment opportunity for individuals seeking both financial returns and environmental impact. In this subchapter, we will delve into the world of renewable energy private placements, exploring the various ways investors can participate in this sector and capitalize on its potential.

Private placements offer a unique avenue for investors to access exclusive opportunities that are not readily available on public markets. This subchapter aims to provide insight into how investors can navigate the renewable energy private placement landscape and make informed investment decisions.

Investing in renewable energy private placements requires a thorough understanding of the sector's dynamics and the specific risks and opportunities it presents. This subchapter will explore the key drivers of the renewable energy industry, such as government policies, technological advancements, and changing consumer preferences. It will also shed light on the various subsectors within renewable energy, including solar, wind, hydro, geothermal, and biomass, offering investors a comprehensive overview of the available opportunities.

Furthermore, we will discuss the benefits and considerations of investing in renewable energy private placements, with a focus on risk management, expected returns, and liquidity. Understanding these aspects is crucial for investors to align their investment goals with the potential rewards and risks associated with renewable energy projects.

To cater to the diverse interests of our audience, we will also explore how investors can specifically invest in renewable energy private placements for real estate, startups, biotech companies, technology firms, healthcare startups, food and beverage businesses, social impact projects, entertainment and media ventures, as well as art and collectibles. Each niche presents unique investment opportunities and requires a tailored approach.

Throughout this subchapter, we will provide concrete examples and case studies that illustrate successful renewable energy private placements and highlight the lessons learned from these experiences. We will also address the due diligence process, including key factors to consider when evaluating investment opportunities, such as project feasibility, management team expertise, and financial projections.

By the end of this subchapter, investors will have a solid foundation to confidently explore and engage in renewable energy private placements. They will be equipped with the necessary knowledge and tools to make informed investment decisions, seize opportunities in this burgeoning sector, and contribute to a sustainable future.

Note: The content provided in this subchapter is for informational purposes only and should not be considered as financial or investment advice. Investors are encouraged to consult with their financial advisors before making any investment decisions.

Evaluating Renewable Energy Investment Opportunities

Investing in renewable energy projects has gained significant popularity in recent years, as the world continues to shift towards a more sustainable and environmentally friendly future. This subchapter aims to provide investors with a comprehensive guide on how to evaluate and make informed decisions when investing in renewable energy opportunities.

When considering renewable energy investments, it is essential to conduct thorough due diligence to assess the viability and potential return on investment. Here are some key factors to consider:

1. Technology and Innovation: Evaluate the technology being used in the renewable energy project. Is it proven, reliable, and scalable? Stay up-to-date with the latest advancements in the field to identify projects that utilize cutting-edge technologies.

2. Regulatory Environment: Understand the regulatory landscape surrounding renewable energy. Investigate government policies, incentives, and subsidies that may impact the project's profitability. Assess the stability of the regulatory framework to mitigate potential risks.

3. Market Analysis: Conduct a comprehensive market analysis to identify the demand for renewable energy in the target market. Evaluate factors such as energy consumption patterns, government initiatives, and consumer preferences to gauge the project's long-term sustainability.

4. Financial Viability: Analyze the financial aspects of the investment opportunity, including revenue potential, operating expenses, and cash flow projections. Evaluate the project's financial stability, profitability, and potential risks.

5. Environmental Impact: Assess the project's environmental impact by analyzing its carbon footprint, energy efficiency, and contribution to reducing greenhouse gas emissions. Investors increasingly prioritize projects that align with sustainable development goals.

6. Project Management Team: Evaluate the expertise and track record of the project's management team. Look for individuals with relevant experience in the renewable energy sector, as this can significantly impact the project's success.

7. Risk Assessment: Identify and evaluate potential risks associated with the investment, such as regulatory changes, technological obsolescence, and market volatility. Construct a risk mitigation strategy to protect your investment.

By considering these factors, investors can make informed decisions when evaluating renewable energy investment opportunities. It is crucial to research and stay informed about the latest developments in the renewable energy sector to identify emerging trends and promising projects. Remember, investing in renewable energy not only offers financial returns but also contributes to a more sustainable and greener future for generations to come.

Due Diligence for Renewable Energy Private Placements

Investing in renewable energy projects through private placements offers a unique opportunity to both diversify your investment portfolio and contribute to a sustainable future. However, before diving into these exclusive opportunities, it is crucial to conduct thorough due diligence to ensure you make informed investment decisions. This subchapter will guide you through the essential aspects of due diligence specifically tailored to renewable energy private placements.

1. Understanding the Project: Start by delving into the details of the renewable energy project you are considering. Assess the technology used, the project's location, and its potential for generating clean energy. Evaluate the project's long-term viability and its alignment with your investment goals.

2. Management Team Expertise: Evaluate the experience and track record of the management team responsible for executing the renewable energy project. Look for individuals with a proven background in the renewable energy industry, as their expertise will be crucial in ensuring project success.

3. Regulatory Landscape: Familiarize yourself with the regulatory environment surrounding renewable energy projects in the specific jurisdiction where the project is located. Understand any applicable permits, licenses, and incentives that may impact the project's financial performance.

4. Financial Analysis: Perform a comprehensive financial analysis of the project, including revenue projections, cost structures, and potential risks. Assess the project's financial viability and compare it to industry benchmarks to gauge its potential for generating returns.

5. Environmental Impact: Evaluate the project's environmental impact, including its carbon footprint and contribution to reducing greenhouse gas emissions. Ensure that the project aligns with your values and meets the sustainability objectives you have set for your investment portfolio.

6. Risk Assessment: Identify and assess the risks associated with the renewable energy project. Evaluate factors such as construction delays, technological challenges, regulatory changes, and potential market fluctuations. Consider how these risks could impact the project's financial performance and your investment.

7. Legal Considerations: Engage legal professionals to review all legal documents related to the private placement, including offering memorandums, subscription agreements, and partnership

agreements. Ensure that your interests are adequately protected and that all necessary legal requirements are met.

By conducting thorough due diligence on renewable energy private placements, you can mitigate potential risks and make informed investment decisions. Remember, investing in renewable energy not only offers potential financial returns but also contributes to a sustainable future.

Investment Strategies for Renewable Energy Private Placements

As the world continues to prioritize sustainable energy solutions, investing in renewable energy projects has become an attractive opportunity for investors. Private placements offer an exclusive avenue for investing in these projects, providing investors with the potential for significant returns while contributing to a greener future. In this subchapter, we will explore the investment strategies for renewable energy private placements, equipping you with the knowledge to make informed investment decisions in this niche.

1. Understand the Renewable Energy Landscape: Before diving into private placements, it is crucial to familiarize yourself with the renewable energy sector. Stay updated on the latest trends, technologies, and government policies that impact the industry. This knowledge will help you identify promising investment opportunities and evaluate their potential risks.

2. Conduct Thorough Due Diligence: Private placements require diligent research and analysis. Evaluate the track record of the renewable energy project and the management team behind it. Assess the project's financials, market potential, and competitive advantage. Engage with experts or seek professional advice to ensure

you have a comprehensive understanding of the investment opportunity.

3. Diversify Your Portfolio: It is wise to diversify your investments across different renewable energy projects. By spreading your capital across multiple projects, you mitigate the risk of any single investment underperforming. Consider investing in various renewable energy sectors, such as solar, wind, hydro, biomass, or geothermal, to further diversify your portfolio.

4. Assess the Project's Environmental Impact: Renewable energy investments often appeal to investors seeking both financial returns and positive environmental impact. Evaluate the project's potential to reduce greenhouse gas emissions, promote clean energy generation, and contribute to sustainable development. This assessment will allow you to align your investment choices with your values and goals.

5. Stay Informed About Tax Incentives and Subsidies: Governments worldwide offer various tax incentives and subsidies to promote renewable energy projects. Stay updated on these incentives as they can significantly impact the financial viability of the investment. Consult with tax professionals or experts in renewable energy finance to understand the intricacies and potential benefits of these incentives.

6. Consider Co-Investment Opportunities: Private placements in renewable energy projects often offer co-investment opportunities. By joining forces with other investors, you can pool resources and share risks, increasing the likelihood of success. Evaluate the co-investment options available and consider partnering with like-minded investors to maximize your returns and impact.

Investing in renewable energy private placements can provide investors with both financial returns and the satisfaction of supporting environmentally-friendly projects. By following these investment strategies and staying informed about the renewable energy market, you can make well-informed investment decisions and contribute to a sustainable future.

Chapter 6: Investing in Private Placements for Art and Collectibles

Overview of Art and Collectibles Private Placements

Private placements offer unique investment opportunities that are not available to the general public. They provide a way for accredited investors to participate in exclusive investment offerings, including those in the art and collectibles market. This subchapter will provide an overview of art and collectibles private placements, highlighting their benefits, risks, and potential returns.

Art and collectibles private placements involve investing in tangible assets such as paintings, sculptures, rare coins, antique furniture, and other valuable items. These investments offer several advantages for investors seeking diversification and potential high returns. One of the key benefits is the potential for significant appreciation over time, as the value of art and collectibles can increase due to factors such as scarcity, historical significance, and demand from wealthy collectors.

Investing in art and collectibles private placements also allows investors to access a market that has historically shown resilience during economic downturns. Unlike traditional financial assets, the value of art and collectibles is less influenced by market fluctuations and can provide a hedge against inflation. Additionally, these investments can offer a unique level of personal enjoyment and satisfaction, as investors may have the opportunity to own and display the artwork or collectibles they invest in.

However, it is important to note that investing in art and collectibles private placements carries certain risks. The market for these assets can be highly subjective and illiquid, meaning that it may be difficult to sell the investment at a desired price or timeframe. The value of art and collectibles is also subject to changing tastes and trends, which can impact their marketability and value. Furthermore, determining the true value of these assets can be challenging, as it often requires expertise and knowledge of the market.

Potential returns from art and collectibles private placements can vary widely depending on the specific investment and market conditions. While some investments may yield substantial profits, others may not perform as expected. It is crucial for investors to conduct thorough due diligence, including assessing the reputation and track record of the art dealer or collectibles expert managing the private placement.

In conclusion, art and collectibles private placements offer investors the opportunity to diversify their portfolios and potentially benefit from the appreciation of tangible assets. However, these investments come with risks and require careful consideration. By understanding the market dynamics, conducting thorough due diligence, and seeking advice from experts, investors can make informed decisions when investing in art and collectibles private placements.

Assessing Art and Collectibles Investment Opportunities

Investing in art and collectibles can be a lucrative endeavor for investors who have a keen eye for value and a passion for the arts. In this subchapter, we will explore the various factors to consider when assessing art and collectibles investment opportunities.

1. Market Analysis: Before investing in art and collectibles, it is crucial to conduct a thorough market analysis. This includes studying historical sales data, monitoring trends, and staying updated on the current market conditions. Understanding the demand and supply dynamics of the art market will help investors make informed decisions.

2. Expert Opinion: Seek advice from art experts, curators, and dealers who have a deep understanding of the art and collectibles market. Their insights and expertise can provide valuable guidance in assessing the potential investment opportunities. Additionally, consulting with specialists in specific niches, such as contemporary art or antique furniture, can help investors gain an edge in their investment strategy.

3. Provenance and Authentication: Authenticity is a critical factor when investing in art and collectibles. Ensuring that the artwork or collectible item has a verifiable provenance and comes with proper documentation is essential. Engaging the services of reputable authentication experts or institutions can provide peace of mind and safeguard against fraudulent investments.

4. Rarity and Condition: Rarity and condition play a significant role in determining the value of art and collectibles. Rare or limited-edition pieces tend to appreciate in value over time. Additionally, the condition of the artwork or collectible item can greatly impact its

marketability and future value. Investors should carefully assess the condition and rarity of the pieces they are considering.

5. Diversification: As with any investment strategy, diversification is key. Investing in a portfolio of art and collectibles across various genres, periods, and mediums can help mitigate risk and maximize potential returns. By diversifying their investments, investors can spread their risk and capitalize on different market trends.

6. Exit Strategy: Before investing, it is important to have a well-defined exit strategy. Art and collectibles are illiquid assets, and selling them can often take time. Investors should consider whether they plan to hold the investment long-term or sell it in the future. Understanding the potential challenges and timeframes involved in the selling process is crucial for a successful investment.

In conclusion, assessing art and collectibles investment opportunities requires a combination of market analysis, expert opinion, and a thorough understanding of the specific niche. By conducting due diligence, diversifying investments, and having a clear exit strategy, investors can navigate the art and collectibles market with confidence and potentially reap significant rewards.

Conducting Due Diligence for Art and Collectibles Private Placements

Investing in private placements can offer exclusive opportunities across various industries, including art and collectibles. Art and collectibles have gained considerable attention as alternative investments, with the potential for significant returns. However, investing in this niche requires careful due diligence to ensure a successful investment. In this subchapter, we will explore the key factors to consider when conducting due diligence for art and collectibles private placements.

1. Market Analysis: Begin by understanding the overall market for art and collectibles. Analyze recent trends, sales data, and pricing patterns to gain insights into the potential growth and risks associated with investing in this market.

2. Expertise and Reputation: Look for private placement opportunities that are backed by reputable experts in the art and collectibles industry. Assess their track record, experience, and knowledge to ensure that they have a deep understanding of the market and can guide your investment decisions effectively.

3. Authenticity and Provenance: Art and collectibles are susceptible to counterfeiting and fraud. Verify the authenticity and provenance of the pieces being offered for investment. Thoroughly examine the documentation, provenance history, and any certificates of authenticity to minimize the risk of purchasing counterfeit items.

4. Valuation and Appraisal: Seek independent appraisals and valuations from trusted professionals to ensure that the investment is priced fairly. This will help you gauge the potential for appreciation and make informed investment decisions.

5. Insurance and Storage: Insure the art and collectibles to safeguard against potential risks such as theft, damage, or loss. Additionally, consider the storage and maintenance requirements of the pieces to preserve their value over time.

6. Exit Strategy: Understand the exit options available for your investment. Private placements in art and collectibles can have longer holding periods, so it's crucial to have a clear understanding of how and when you can liquidate your investment if needed.

7. Regulatory Compliance: Ensure that the private placement opportunity complies with all relevant regulations and legal requirements. Verify that the investment is structured in a manner that protects your rights as an investor.

Investing in art and collectibles through private placements can be an exciting and potentially lucrative venture. However, it is crucial to conduct thorough due diligence to mitigate risks and maximize returns. By following these key steps, investors can make informed decisions and navigate the unique nuances of this niche investment market.

Investment Strategies for Art and Collectibles Private Placements

Investing in art and collectibles has long been considered an alternative investment strategy, offering investors the opportunity to diversify their portfolios and potentially achieve significant returns. Private placements in the art and collectibles market provide an exclusive avenue for investors to participate in this lucrative market, and this subchapter will explore the strategies and considerations associated with investing in art and collectibles private placements. When it comes to investing in art and collectibles private placements, it is essential for investors to conduct thorough due diligence. This involves researching the artwork or collectible, evaluating its historical performance, assessing its market demand and potential for appreciation, and understanding the reputation and expertise of the issuer or investment manager. By understanding these factors, investors can make informed decisions and mitigate potential risks.

Furthermore, investors should consider diversifying their art and collectibles investments by allocating funds across different asset classes, such as paintings, sculptures, rare coins, vintage automobiles, or even rare stamps. By diversifying their holdings, investors can reduce the impact of individual artwork fluctuations and protect their investment capital.

Another key strategy for investing in art and collectibles private placements is to leverage the expertise of professionals in the field.

Engaging the services of art consultants, appraisers, or investment advisors specializing in art and collectibles can provide invaluable insights and guidance. These professionals possess deep industry knowledge and can help identify promising investment opportunities, negotiate favorable terms, and ensure the authenticity and provenance of the artworks.

Investors should also consider the liquidity and exit strategies associated with art and collectibles private placements. Unlike traditional investments, the art market can be less liquid and subject to fluctuations in demand. Therefore, investors should have a clear plan in place for how and when they intend to sell their investments. This might involve partnering with galleries, auction houses, or private collectors who have access to potential buyers.

Lastly, investors interested in art and collectibles private placements should stay abreast of market trends, industry news, and regulatory developments. The art market is dynamic and influenced by various factors, including economic conditions, cultural shifts, and changes in taste and preferences. By staying informed, investors can make timely investment decisions and capitalize on emerging opportunities.

In conclusion, investing in art and collectibles private placements can be a rewarding venture for investors seeking to diversify their portfolios and explore alternative investment strategies. By conducting thorough due diligence, diversifying holdings, leveraging professional expertise, planning exit strategies, and staying informed, investors can maximize their chances of success in this exclusive market.

Chapter 7: Investing in Private Placements for

Technology Companies

Introduction to Technology Private Placements

In today's rapidly evolving world, technology plays a crucial role in shaping industries and driving innovation. As an investor, it is essential to stay ahead of the curve and explore opportunities that offer high growth potential. One such avenue is investing in technology private placements, which provide exclusive opportunities to capitalize on the advancements in various sectors. Private placements, also known as private offerings, are investment opportunities offered to a select group of individuals or institutions. These opportunities allow investors to participate in the growth of promising technology companies that are not yet publicly traded. By investing in private placements, investors gain access to companies at an early stage, often before they have achieved widespread recognition.

Investing in technology private placements offers several advantages. Firstly, it allows investors to diversify their portfolios by adding exposure to the technology sector. With technology becoming increasingly integral to all industries, investing in technology companies provides a unique avenue for potential high returns.

Furthermore, technology private placements offer opportunities to invest in specific niches within the technology sector. Whether it be investing in startups, biotech companies, renewable energy projects, art and collectibles, healthcare startups, or entertainment and media ventures, there is a wide range of options available to suit individual investment preferences.

Investing in technology private placements also allows investors to align their investments with their values. For those interested in social impact projects or renewable energy, private placements provide a means to support businesses that are making a positive difference in society.

However, it is crucial to note that investing in private placements comes with risks. These investments are typically illiquid, meaning they cannot be easily sold or traded on the public market. Additionally, the lack of public information and regulatory oversight can make it challenging to evaluate the potential risks and rewards accurately. Therefore, it is essential for investors to conduct thorough due diligence and work with experienced professionals who can guide them through the investment process.

In conclusion, technology private placements offer investors a unique opportunity to participate in the growth and success of promising technology companies. By diversifying their portfolios and investing in specific niches within the technology sector, investors can potentially achieve high returns while supporting innovative businesses. However, it is crucial for investors to approach these opportunities with caution and seek professional guidance to navigate the complexities of private placements successfully.

Analyzing Technology Investment Opportunities

In today's fast-paced world, technology investment opportunities have become increasingly popular among investors seeking high returns. From startups revolutionizing industries to biotech breakthroughs and renewable energy projects, technology companies offer a wide range of investment options. This subchapter aims to guide investors interested in technology-focused private placements, providing insights into various sectors and highlighting key factors to consider before making investment decisions.

Investing in private placements can be an excellent way to diversify your portfolio and gain exposure to exciting technology ventures. However, it is crucial to approach these opportunities with caution and conduct thorough analysis. Understanding the market dynamics, assessing the company's potential, and evaluating the risks involved are essential steps in this process.

For those interested in investing in private placements for technology companies, it is vital to evaluate the company's innovation, competitive advantage, and scalability. Examining their intellectual property portfolio, market traction, and management team expertise can provide valuable insights into the company's growth potential.

Investing in private placements for biotech companies requires a different set of considerations. Investors in this niche must assess the company's clinical trial progress, regulatory approvals, and potential market demand for their products. Understanding the biotech landscape, including competition and upcoming trends, is also crucial in making informed investment decisions.

Similarly, when investing in renewable energy projects, investors should analyze factors such as the project's location, technology used, and potential environmental impact. Evaluating the financial viability, regulatory landscape, and long-term sustainability goals of the project are vital steps in assessing the investment opportunity.

Technology investment opportunities are not limited to traditional sectors. The art and collectibles market, for example, have seen a surge in digital platforms and blockchain technology. Understanding the intersection between technology and art can help investors identify innovative platforms and projects that aim to revolutionize this industry.

Regardless of the sector, investors should also consider the impact of their investments. Private placements for social impact projects, healthcare startups, and food and beverage businesses offer opportunities to align financial goals with societal and environmental benefits. Assessing the social and environmental impact of these projects can provide investors with a sense of purpose and contribute to positive change.

In conclusion, analyzing technology investment opportunities requires thorough market research, understanding of the specific sector, and evaluation of key factors. Whether investing in startups, biotech companies, renewable energy projects, or social impact ventures, investors should carefully analyze the potential risks and rewards. By doing so, investors can position themselves to benefit from the dynamic and ever-evolving world of technology investments while making a positive impact on society.

Due Diligence for Technology Private Placements

Investing in private placements can be an exciting opportunity to gain access to exclusive investment options that are not available to the general public. However, before diving into any private placement investment, it is crucial for investors to conduct thorough due diligence to minimize risks and maximize potential returns. This subchapter will focus on the due diligence process specifically for technology private placements.

Technology companies are known for their rapid advancements and potential for high growth, making them attractive investment opportunities. However, investing in technology private placements requires careful evaluation of various aspects to make informed investment decisions.

The first step in due diligence for technology private placements is to research the company's background and track record. Investors should examine the company's history, management team, and their expertise in the technology sector. Assessing the management team's experience and previous successes can provide valuable insights into the company's potential for success.

Next, investors should analyze the technology itself. Understanding the product or service, its uniqueness, and competitive advantages are crucial. Investors should consider the market demand, potential for scalability, and any intellectual property protection the company may have. Additionally, evaluating the company's research and development capabilities is essential to ensure ongoing innovation and competitiveness.

Financial due diligence is another critical aspect of the process. Investors should review the company's financial statements, including balance sheets, income statements, and cash flow statements. This analysis helps investors assess the company's financial health, profitability, and growth potential.

Furthermore, investors should evaluate the company's market position and competitive landscape. Analyzing the industry trends, market size, and potential competitors can provide insights into the company's ability to capture market share and sustain growth.

Lastly, investors should consider any legal and regulatory factors that may impact the technology company. Understanding the regulatory environment, potential legal risks, and compliance with industry standards is essential to mitigate any legal liabilities.

In conclusion, conducting due diligence for technology private placements is crucial to make informed investment decisions. By thoroughly researching the company's background, evaluating the technology, analyzing financials, assessing market position, and considering legal factors, investors can minimize risks and maximize potential returns in the technology sector.

Investment Strategies for Technology Private Placements

In today's fast-paced and ever-evolving world, technology private placements offer investors a unique opportunity to tap into the potential of innovative companies that are driving advancements in various industries. Investing in technology private placements can be a lucrative endeavor, but it requires careful consideration and a well-thought-out strategy. This subchapter will provide valuable insights and guidance on investment strategies specifically tailored for technology private placements.

1. Conduct Thorough Due Diligence: Before investing in any technology private placement, it is crucial to conduct extensive due diligence. This involves researching the company's management team, financials, competitive landscape, and growth potential. Understanding the technology being developed and its market viability is essential.

2. Diversify Your Portfolio: Investing in technology private placements should be part of a well-diversified portfolio. By spreading your investments across different technology sectors, such as software, hardware, biotech, or renewable energy projects, you can mitigate risk and maximize potential returns.

3. Seek Professional Advice: Investing in technology private placements can be complex, especially for those new to the field. Seeking advice from experienced professionals, such as financial advisors or venture capitalists specializing in technology investments, can help you navigate the intricacies of this market.

4. Stay Updated on Technological Advancements: Technology is constantly evolving, and staying informed about the latest trends and innovations is crucial for successful investing. Subscribing to industry publications, attending conferences, and joining technology-focused investment networks can provide valuable insights and potential investment opportunities.

5. Consider Long-Term Growth: Technology private placements, particularly in sectors like biotech or renewable energy, often require a longer investment horizon. Investing with a long-term growth mindset can help you capitalize on the potential of breakthrough technologies and their impact on various industries.

6. Evaluate Exit Strategies: Before investing, it is essential to evaluate potential exit strategies. This could include initial public offerings (IPOs), mergers and acquisitions, or secondary private placements. Understanding the company's plans for future liquidity events can help you make informed investment decisions.

Investing in technology private placements can be a rewarding venture, but it requires a strategic approach. By conducting thorough due diligence, diversifying your portfolio, seeking professional advice, staying updated on technological advancements, considering long-term growth, and evaluating exit strategies, you can increase your chances of success in this exciting investment niche.

Whether you are interested in investing in technology private placements for real estate, startups, biotech companies, renewable energy projects, or any other niche, these strategies will provide a solid foundation for making informed investment decisions. Remember, technology is at the forefront of innovation, and by investing in the right companies, you can be part of the transformative changes shaping our future.

Chapter 8: Investing in Private Placements for Healthcare Startups

Overview of Healthcare Private Placements

Private placements are exclusive investment opportunities that offer investors the chance to invest in various sectors, including healthcare. This subchapter will provide an overview of healthcare private placements and how investors can tap into this lucrative market. Whether you are interested in healthcare startups, biotech companies, or renewable energy projects within the healthcare industry, private placements can offer unique investment prospects. Healthcare private placements provide investors with access to a range of investment options, allowing them to support innovative companies and projects within the healthcare sector. These opportunities span various niches, such as biotech, renewable energy, technology, and more. Investors can choose to invest in healthcare startups, which often focus on developing cutting-edge medical technologies and solutions. These startups usually require funding to support research and development, clinical trials, and market expansion.

Investing in private placements for biotech companies is another exciting option within the healthcare sector. Biotech companies are at the forefront of medical advancements, working on developing new drugs, therapies, and medical devices. By investing in these companies through private placements, investors can contribute to the development of breakthrough treatments and potentially earn significant returns on their investments.

Renewable energy projects within the healthcare industry are also gaining traction. As sustainability and environmental consciousness become increasingly important, more healthcare organizations are adopting renewable energy solutions. Investing in private placements for renewable energy projects in healthcare enables investors to support the transition to clean energy while potentially reaping financial rewards.

Moreover, private placements offer opportunities to invest in healthcare projects related to art and collectibles, food and beverage businesses, social impact projects, entertainment and media ventures, and technology companies. These diverse investment options cater to the specific interests and preferences of individual investors.

Investing in healthcare private placements requires careful consideration and due diligence. Potential investors should thoroughly research the companies or projects they are considering, assessing factors such as market potential, management team expertise, and financial stability. It is also recommended to consult with financial advisors or professionals well-versed in private placements to mitigate risks and maximize investment potential.

In conclusion, healthcare private placements offer a unique avenue for investors to support and profit from the dynamic healthcare industry. Whether investing in startups, biotech companies, renewable energy projects, or other healthcare ventures, private placements provide exclusive opportunities to contribute to innovation and potentially earn attractive returns on investments.

Evaluating Healthcare Investment Opportunities

The healthcare sector has long been considered a lucrative area for investment, with its potential for sizable returns and the opportunity to make a positive impact on people's lives. However, evaluating healthcare investment opportunities can be a complex task, requiring a thorough understanding of the industry and the factors that drive success in this sector. In this subchapter, we will explore the key considerations and strategies for evaluating healthcare investment opportunities.

1. Industry Analysis: Before investing in any healthcare opportunity, it is crucial to conduct a comprehensive analysis of the industry. This involves examining market trends, regulatory environment, competitive landscape, and potential risks. Understanding the dynamics of the healthcare market will help you identify opportunities that are well-positioned for growth.

2. Investment Thesis: Developing a clear investment thesis is essential to guide your decision-making process. Define your investment goals and objectives, and assess how the opportunity aligns with your investment strategy. Consider factors such as the potential for revenue growth, scalability, competitive advantage, and the overall market opportunity.

3. Team and Management: Evaluate the expertise and experience of the management team behind the healthcare opportunity. Look for individuals with a track record of success in the healthcare industry, as well as a deep understanding of the specific niche within healthcare you are investing in. A strong management team is crucial for executing the business plan and driving growth.

4. Market Potential: Assess the market potential for the healthcare investment opportunity. Consider factors such as the size of the

target market, the demand for the product or service, and the competitive landscape. Evaluate the scalability of the opportunity and its potential for expansion into new markets.

5. Financials and Valuation: Analyze the financials of the healthcare opportunity, including revenue projections, profitability, and cash flow. Assess the valuation of the investment opportunity to ensure that it is reasonable and provides an attractive return on investment.

6. Risk Assessment: Evaluate the risks associated with the healthcare investment opportunity, including regulatory risks, reimbursement risks, and competitive risks. Consider the potential impact of these risks on the investment's viability and the strategies in place to mitigate them.

7. Due Diligence: Conduct thorough due diligence to validate the claims and assumptions made by the healthcare opportunity. This may involve reviewing financial statements, conducting site visits, and speaking with industry experts. Ensure that all necessary legal and regulatory requirements are met.

8. Diversification: Consider diversifying your healthcare investment portfolio across different sub-sectors within the healthcare industry. This will help mitigate risks and increase the potential for overall returns.

In conclusion, evaluating healthcare investment opportunities requires a deep understanding of the industry and careful analysis of various factors. By conducting thorough due diligence, assessing market potential, and considering the expertise of the management team, investors can make informed decisions and maximize their chances of success in this promising sector.

Due Diligence for Healthcare Private Placements

Investing in private placements offers unique opportunities to investors across various niches, including real estate, startups, biotech companies, renewable energy projects, art and collectibles, technology companies, healthcare startups, food and beverage businesses, social impact projects, and entertainment and media ventures. This subchapter will focus on the due diligence process specifically for healthcare private placements, providing investors with valuable insights to make informed investment decisions in this sector.

When investing in healthcare private placements, thorough due diligence is critical to mitigate risks and maximize potential returns. Here are key factors to consider during the due diligence process:

1. Industry Analysis: Gain a deep understanding of the healthcare sector, including market trends, regulatory environment, competitive landscape, and potential risks. Evaluate the growth potential and long-term viability of the healthcare private placement opportunity.

2. Management Team: Assess the experience, track record, and expertise of the healthcare private placement's management team. Look for a team with a proven history in the healthcare industry, as well as a clear strategic vision for the company.

3. Intellectual Property: Evaluate the strength and uniqueness of the healthcare private placement's intellectual property, such as patents, trademarks, or proprietary technologies. Intellectual property can significantly impact the company's competitive advantage and potential for future growth.

4. Financial Analysis: Scrutinize the financial statements, revenue projections, and cash flow forecasts of the healthcare private

placement. Assess the company's financial health, profitability, and ability to generate sustainable returns.

5. Regulatory Compliance: Ensure that the healthcare private placement adheres to all relevant regulations and compliance requirements. This includes assessing the company's licensing, certifications, and any potential legal or regulatory risks.

6. Competitive Landscape: Analyze the competitive environment within the healthcare industry and the healthcare private placement's position in the market. Identify potential competitors and evaluate the company's unique value proposition.

7. Risk Assessment: Conduct a thorough risk assessment, considering factors such as market volatility, technological advancements, reimbursement policies, and regulatory changes. Understand the potential risks and their impact on the healthcare private placement's performance.

8. Exit Strategy: Evaluate the healthcare private placement's exit strategy, such as potential IPOs, acquisitions, or mergers. Assess the likelihood and potential returns of the exit strategy to determine the investment's liquidity.

By conducting rigorous due diligence and considering these key factors, investors can make well-informed decisions when investing in healthcare private placements. This process helps to identify opportunities with strong growth potential, solid management teams, and sustainable competitive advantages. Remember, investing in private placements carries inherent risks, and it is crucial to consult with professionals and conduct thorough research before making any investment decisions.

Investment Strategies for Healthcare Private Placements

Private placements offer investors a unique opportunity to invest in exclusive opportunities that are not available through traditional public markets. This subchapter will provide valuable insights into investment strategies specifically tailored for healthcare private placements. Whether you are interested in investing in biotech companies, healthcare startups, or renewable energy projects, this guide will equip you with the knowledge and strategies to make informed investment decisions in the healthcare sector.

1. Conduct Thorough Due Diligence: Before investing in any healthcare private placement opportunity, it is crucial to conduct comprehensive due diligence. Evaluate the company's financials, management team, competitive landscape, and growth potential. Assess the industry's regulatory environment and any potential risks associated with the investment.

2. Seek Expert Advice: Investing in healthcare private placements can be complex and requires specialized knowledge. Consider working with experienced advisors who have a deep understanding of the healthcare industry. Their expertise can help you navigate the unique challenges and opportunities in this sector.

3. Diversify Your Portfolio: As with any investment strategy, diversification is key. Spread your investments across different healthcare sectors, such as biotech, technology companies, healthcare startups, and renewable energy projects. This will help mitigate risk and potentially maximize returns.

4. Stay Informed: Stay updated on the latest trends and developments in the healthcare industry. Follow industry publications, attend conferences, and join online communities to stay informed about new opportunities in healthcare private placements.

Being knowledgeable about the industry will enable you to identify potential investment opportunities and make well-informed decisions.

5. Understand the Exit Strategy: Before investing, it is essential to understand the exit strategy of the private placement. Will the company eventually go public, or will it be acquired by a larger player in the industry? Understanding the potential exit options will help you evaluate the long-term viability and potential returns of your investment.

6. Consider Social Impact Projects: Healthcare private placements offer a unique opportunity to invest in projects that have a positive social impact. Consider investing in healthcare startups focused on addressing critical healthcare challenges or renewable energy projects that contribute to a sustainable future. Investing in socially responsible projects can provide both financial returns and a sense of fulfillment.

Investing in healthcare private placements can be lucrative and rewarding for investors. However, it requires careful consideration, due diligence, and a comprehensive understanding of the industry. By following these investment strategies, you can navigate the healthcare private placement market with confidence and potentially unlock exclusive investment opportunities in the healthcare sector.

Chapter 9: Investing in Private Placements for Food and Beverage Businesses

Introduction to Food and Beverage Private Placements

Welcome to the subchapter on "Introduction to Food and Beverage Private Placements" from the book "Private Placements Unveiled: A Guide to Investing in Exclusive Opportunities." In this section, we will explore the exciting world of private placements in the food and beverage industry, providing valuable insights for investors interested in this niche.

Investing in private placements offers unique opportunities to gain exposure and potentially earn significant returns in specific industries. The food and beverage sector is one such industry that has captured the attention of savvy investors looking to diversify their portfolios. With the increasing demand for innovative food products, sustainable agriculture, health-conscious options, and unique dining experiences, the food and beverage industry presents attractive investment prospects.

Private placements in the food and beverage industry provide investors with an exclusive chance to participate in the growth and success of various businesses in this sector. These placements involve investing capital directly into privately-held food and beverage companies, ranging from startups to established businesses looking to expand their operations. By investing in private placements, investors can support promising ventures and potentially benefit from their future success.

Investing in food and beverage private placements offers several advantages. Firstly, it allows investors to tap into a sector that has demonstrated resilience and stability even during economic downturns. People will always need food, making this industry relatively recession-proof. Additionally, investing in private placements allows investors to access unique opportunities that are not available through traditional public markets.

This subchapter will provide a comprehensive overview of how to invest in private placements specifically within the food and beverage industry. We will explore the different types of private placements available, including those tailored for real estate ventures, startups, biotech companies, renewable energy projects, art and collectibles, technology companies, healthcare startups, social impact projects, and entertainment and media ventures.

We will discuss the key considerations for investors, such as evaluating the potential growth and profitability of food and beverage businesses, assessing the management team, understanding the risks involved, and conducting due diligence. Additionally, we will delve into the various investment structures, such as equity investments, debt investments, and convertible notes, and their implications for investors.

By the end of this subchapter, investors will have a solid understanding of the opportunities and challenges associated with investing in food and beverage private placements. Whether you are a seasoned investor or new to the world of private placements, this subchapter will equip you with the knowledge and insights necessary to make informed investment decisions in the dynamic and ever-evolving food and beverage industry.

Assessing Food and Beverage Investment Opportunities

Investing in the food and beverage industry can be an exciting and profitable venture for investors looking to diversify their portfolio. This subchapter aims to provide valuable insights and guidance on how to assess and evaluate food and beverage investment opportunities. Whether you are interested in investing in established businesses or startups within this industry, this section will equip you with the necessary knowledge to make informed investment decisions.

When evaluating food and beverage investment opportunities, it is essential to consider various factors. Firstly, conducting thorough market research is crucial. Understanding the current trends, consumer preferences, and market demand for specific food and beverage products is essential. This will help you identify potential investment opportunities and make informed decisions about which sectors or niches to invest in.

In addition to market research, analyzing the financials of the potential investment is vital. This includes studying the company's revenue growth, profitability, and cash flow. Investing in businesses with sustainable and consistent financial performance is usually a wise choice. It is also important to assess the management team's experience and track record in the food and beverage industry. A strong and capable team can greatly contribute to the success of the investment.

Furthermore, investors should consider the competitive landscape of the food and beverage industry. Assessing the strengths and weaknesses of competing businesses can help identify the unique selling points and potential market gaps that the investment opportunity can capitalize on. Additionally, evaluating the scalability and growth potential of the business is crucial. This involves assessing factors such as production capacity, distribution channels, and potential for expansion into new markets.

Investors should also consider the regulatory environment and any potential risks associated with investing in the food and beverage industry. This includes compliance with food safety regulations, labeling requirements, and any potential health or environmental risks. Conducting due diligence and seeking professional advice can help mitigate these risks and ensure a successful investment.

Lastly, it is important for investors to align their investment goals with the social impact and sustainability aspects of the food and beverage industry. Investing in businesses that promote ethical sourcing, sustainable practices, and social responsibility can not only generate financial returns but also contribute to positive societal and environmental change.

In conclusion, assessing food and beverage investment opportunities requires a comprehensive analysis of market trends, financials, management capabilities, competitive landscape, regulatory environment, and social impact factors. By carefully evaluating these aspects, investors can make informed decisions and capitalize on the potential opportunities within the food and beverage industry.

Conducting Due Diligence for Food and Beverage Private Placements

When it comes to investing in private placements, conducting thorough due diligence is crucial. This is especially true for the food and beverage industry, which is known for its unique challenges and complexities. In this subchapter, we will explore the key factors to consider when conducting due diligence for food and beverage private placements.

1. Market Analysis: Start by analyzing the current market trends and conditions in the food and beverage industry. Look for growth opportunities, emerging consumer preferences, and potential competition. Understanding the market dynamics will help you assess the viability and potential profitability of the investment.

2. Management Team: The success of any food and beverage business heavily relies on the expertise and experience of the

management team. Evaluate their track record, industry knowledge, and ability to execute the business plan. A strong and experienced team increases the likelihood of success.

3. Business Model and Competitive Advantage: Assess the business model of the company seeking funding. Determine whether it has a unique selling proposition or a competitive advantage that sets it apart from existing players in the market. Understanding the company's value proposition will help you gauge its potential for success.

4. Financial Analysis: Analyze the financials of the company, including revenue projections, historical performance, and cash flow statements. Assess the company's ability to generate consistent profits and its financial stability. Look for signs of financial health, such as positive cash flow and a strong balance sheet.

5. Regulatory and Compliance Considerations: The food and beverage industry is heavily regulated, and compliance with food safety standards and regulations is essential. Ensure that the company has all the necessary licenses, permits, and certifications to operate legally. Assess any potential legal risks or pending litigations that could impact the investment.

6. Supply Chain and Distribution Channels: Examine the company's supply chain and distribution channels. Evaluate the relationships with suppliers, distributors, and retailers. A robust and efficient supply chain is crucial for timely delivery and quality control, which ultimately affects the company's bottom line.

7. Brand Reputation and Customer Loyalty: Assess the company's brand reputation and customer loyalty. Look for customer reviews, feedback, and ratings to gauge customer satisfaction. A strong brand and loyal customer base indicate a higher likelihood of success in the market.

By conducting thorough due diligence in these areas, investors can make informed decisions when investing in food and beverage private placements. Remember that investing in private placements involves risk, and it is always advisable to consult with financial professionals or advisors before making any investment decisions.

Investment Strategies for Food and Beverage Private Placements

Investing in private placements within the food and beverage industry can be an exciting and potentially lucrative opportunity for investors seeking exclusive investment options. This subchapter aims to provide a comprehensive guide on investment strategies tailored specifically for individuals interested in investing in private placements within the food and beverage sector.

First and foremost, it is essential for investors to conduct thorough due diligence on the food and beverage companies they are considering investing in. This involves researching the company's financial performance, market potential, competitive landscape, and management team. Additionally, investors should consider the company's product offerings, target market, and any unique differentiators that may give them a competitive advantage.

One effective investment strategy for food and beverage private placements is to focus on companies that are experiencing significant growth or have the potential for expansion. This can include startups that are disrupting the industry with innovative products or established companies that are looking to expand into new markets or product lines. By investing in companies with growth potential, investors can benefit from the potential for increased valuation and profitability.

Another strategy is to diversify investments within the food and beverage industry. This can involve investing in companies across different subsectors such as organic food, functional beverages, plant-based products, or specialty snacks. By diversifying investments, investors can mitigate risks associated with any one specific company or subsector while capitalizing on the overall growth of the food and beverage industry.

Additionally, investors should consider the social impact and sustainability aspects of the food and beverage companies they invest in. With the increasing demand for ethically sourced and sustainable products, investing in companies that align with these values can provide both financial returns and social impact. This strategy can attract a niche market of conscious consumers, leading to increased brand loyalty and market share.

Furthermore, investors should be aware of the unique challenges and risks associated with the food and beverage industry. These can include changing consumer preferences, intense competition, regulatory hurdles, and supply chain disruptions. It is crucial for investors to assess the company's ability to navigate these challenges successfully and have contingency plans in place.

In conclusion, investing in private placements within the food and beverage industry offers investors an exclusive opportunity to capitalize on the growth and innovation in this sector. By conducting thorough due diligence, focusing on growth potential, diversifying investments, considering social impact, and understanding industry-specific risks, investors can develop effective investment strategies to maximize returns and mitigate risks within the food and beverage private placement market.

Chapter 10: Investing in Private Placements

for Social Impact Projects

Overview of Social Impact Private Placements

In recent years, there has been a growing interest among investors in aligning their investments with their values and making a positive social impact. This has led to the emergence of social impact private placements, which provide investors with an opportunity to support businesses and projects that are focused on addressing social and environmental challenges.

Social impact private placements are a type of investment that allows individuals to invest in companies and projects that prioritize social and environmental goals alongside financial returns. These investments can be made in various industries and sectors, including real estate, startups, biotech, renewable energy, art and collectibles, technology, healthcare, food and beverage, entertainment, and media ventures.

One of the key advantages of investing in social impact private placements is the ability to generate both financial returns and social impact. By investing in companies and projects that are dedicated to creating positive change, investors can contribute to the betterment of society while also potentially earning attractive financial returns. Investing in social impact private placements for real estate allows investors to support affordable housing initiatives, community development projects, or sustainable building practices. Similarly, investing in startups focused on social impact can help fund innovative solutions to pressing social challenges, such as poverty, education, or healthcare.

For those interested in the healthcare sector, investing in social impact private placements can mean supporting startups that are working on breakthrough treatments or medical technologies that have the potential to improve patient outcomes. Similarly, investing in renewable energy projects can help accelerate the transition to clean and sustainable energy sources, reducing carbon emissions and combating climate change.

When it comes to investing in social impact private placements for art and collectibles, investors can support artists and cultural projects that promote diversity, inclusivity, and social awareness.

Furthermore, investing in technology companies focused on social impact can drive advancements in areas such as accessibility, education, or digital inclusion.

It's important to note that investing in social impact private placements requires careful due diligence and understanding of the risks involved. Investors should consider factors such as the track record of the company or project, the potential for financial returns, and the alignment of the investment with their personal values.

In conclusion, social impact private placements offer investors a unique opportunity to make a positive difference in the world while also potentially earning financial returns. Whether it's investing in real estate, startups, biotech, renewable energy, art and collectibles, technology, healthcare, food and beverage, entertainment, or media ventures, there are numerous avenues for investors to support projects and businesses that are dedicated to creating social and environmental impact.

Analyzing Social Impact Investment Opportunities

As the world becomes more socially conscious, investors are increasingly seeking opportunities to make a positive impact while also achieving financial returns. Social impact investment, also known as impact investing, offers a unique avenue for investors to support projects and companies that are dedicated to addressing social and environmental challenges. In this subchapter, we will explore the various social impact investment opportunities available across different sectors.

One of the most prominent sectors for social impact investment is real estate. Investors can invest in private placements that focus on affordable housing initiatives, sustainable development projects, or revitalization of distressed communities. These investments not only generate financial returns but also contribute to the creation of inclusive and sustainable communities.

Startups, particularly those in the technology and healthcare sectors, also offer promising social impact investment opportunities. By investing in early-stage companies that are developing innovative solutions to pressing societal issues, investors can play a pivotal role in driving social change. From healthcare startups working on improving access to quality care to technology companies focused on bridging the digital divide, the potential for impact is significant.

Biotech companies are another attractive niche for social impact investment. By investing in private placements in this sector, investors can support the development of life-saving drugs, medical devices, and therapies that have the potential to transform patients' lives. Renewable energy projects also present compelling opportunities for social impact investors, as they contribute to the transition to a more sustainable and cleaner energy future.

Beyond these sectors, investors can explore private placements in art and collectibles, food and beverage businesses, entertainment and media ventures, and social impact projects. Investing in the arts helps promote cultural diversity and creativity, while supporting food and beverage businesses can have a direct impact on local economies and sustainable farming practices. Furthermore, social impact projects encompass a wide range of initiatives, including education, poverty alleviation, and environmental conservation. When analyzing social impact investment opportunities, it is crucial for investors to consider both the financial and social returns. Conducting thorough due diligence, evaluating the track record of the project or company, and assessing the potential risks are essential steps in the investment process. Additionally, investors should align their investment goals and values with the mission and impact of the project or company they are considering.

In conclusion, analyzing social impact investment opportunities requires a comprehensive understanding of the various sectors and niches available. From real estate and startups to biotech companies and renewable energy projects, investors have a wide range of options to make a positive impact while generating financial returns. By carefully assessing these opportunities and aligning their investment goals with their values, investors can contribute to creating a more sustainable and equitable future.

Due Diligence for Social Impact Private Placements

In recent years, there has been a growing interest among investors in private placements that offer not only financial returns but also positive social and environmental impacts. These investments, known as social impact private placements, allow investors to align their financial goals with their personal values and contribute to meaningful social change. However, before diving into this exciting realm of investment, it is crucial for investors to conduct due diligence and thoroughly evaluate the opportunities at hand. This subchapter will provide a comprehensive guide on how to perform due diligence for social impact private placements across various niches.

When investing in private placements for real estate, investors should carefully assess the project's location, market dynamics, and the developer's track record. They should also evaluate the social impact potential of the development, such as its contribution to affordable housing or sustainable design.

For startups, due diligence should focus on the management team's experience and expertise, the market potential of the product or service, and the scalability of the business model. Additionally, investors should consider the startup's commitment to social impact, such as its mission to address a pressing societal issue.

Similarly, for biotech companies, renewable energy projects, and healthcare startups, due diligence should involve an evaluation of the technology or innovation, the competitive landscape, and the potential impact on society and the environment.

When considering private placements for art and collectibles, investors should assess the authenticity, provenance, and value of the artwork or collectible. They should also examine the artist's reputation and the potential cultural or educational impact of the investment.

For technology companies, due diligence should involve a thorough analysis of the intellectual property, the market demand for the product or service, and the potential societal benefits, such as improving access to education or healthcare.

In the case of food and beverage businesses, investors should consider factors such as the quality and uniqueness of the product, the market potential, and the sustainability practices of the company. Lastly, for social impact projects in entertainment and media ventures, due diligence should focus on the project's alignment with the investor's values, the potential for positive social change, and the financial viability of the venture.

In conclusion, investing in social impact private placements offers investors the opportunity to generate financial returns while making a positive difference in the world. However, it is essential to conduct thorough due diligence across various niches to ensure that the investments align with both financial and social impact goals. By carefully evaluating the opportunities and assessing factors like market dynamics, management team, social impact potential, and financial viability, investors can make informed decisions and contribute to meaningful social change through their investments.

Investment Strategies for Social Impact Private Placements

In recent years, there has been a growing interest among investors to align their investments with their values and make a positive impact on society. This has led to the rise of social impact investing, where investors seek opportunities that generate both financial returns and social or environmental benefits. One avenue that allows investors to participate in social impact investing is through private placements. Private placements offer exclusive investment opportunities that are not available to the general public. They allow individuals to invest directly in companies or projects that are working towards positive social change. Whether you are interested in real estate, startups, biotech, renewable energy, art and collectibles, technology, healthcare, food and beverage, social impact projects, or entertainment and media ventures, private placements can provide you with the chance to invest in these niches for social impact. When considering investment strategies for social impact private placements, it is important to conduct thorough due diligence. Unlike publicly traded companies, private placements are not subject to the same level of regulatory oversight. Therefore, investors must take the time to research and understand the company or project they are considering investing in. This includes reviewing financial statements, business plans, market analysis, and assessing the management team's expertise and track record.

Diversification is another key strategy to consider when investing in social impact private placements. By diversifying your investments across different sectors or industries, you can spread out your risk. This is especially important in the private placement space, where the failure of one investment can have a significant impact on your overall portfolio. Diversifying across various social impact niches can also allow you to support multiple causes or areas of interest.

Furthermore, it is crucial to align your investment goals with the impact you want to create. Each of the niches mentioned - real estate, startups, biotech, renewable energy, art and collectibles, technology, healthcare, food and beverage, social impact projects, and entertainment and media ventures - offers unique opportunities for social change. By identifying the specific social impact you wish to achieve, you can focus your investments in areas that align with your values and maximize the positive change you can make in the world.

Ultimately, investing in social impact private placements requires a combination of financial analysis and a commitment to creating positive change. By carefully selecting investments, diversifying your portfolio, and aligning your goals with the impact you want to make, you can participate in the growing field of social impact investing and contribute to a better future.

Chapter 11: Investing in Private Placements for Entertainment and Media Ventures

Introduction to Entertainment and Media Private Placements

Private placements offer investors a unique opportunity to invest in exclusive ventures across a wide range of industries, including entertainment and media. In this subchapter, we will provide an introduction to entertainment and media private placements, addressing the specific considerations, risks, and potential rewards associated with investing in this niche.

The entertainment and media industry is a dynamic and ever-growing sector that encompasses various sub-sectors such as film, television, music, publishing, gaming, and digital media. Private placements within this industry offer investors the chance to participate in the success of promising ventures, from independent film production companies to streaming platforms revolutionizing the way we consume content.

Investing in entertainment and media private placements requires a thorough understanding of the industry's unique characteristics. One key consideration is the volatile nature of the market, as trends and consumer preferences can change rapidly. Investors must assess the potential for a company's content or platform to resonate with audiences and stand out in a crowded marketplace.

Private placements in entertainment and media also come with inherent risks. The success of a venture can be highly unpredictable, with factors such as competition, changing technologies, and shifts in consumer behavior affecting its profitability. Investors must carefully evaluate the experience and track record of the management team, as well as the company's strategic partnerships and distribution channels, to gauge its potential for success.

However, investing in entertainment and media private placements also offers significant opportunities for high returns. Successful ventures can experience rapid growth and generate substantial revenue, especially in an era where digital platforms have opened up new avenues for content distribution and monetization. Investing in this industry allows investors to support the creation of innovative and impactful content that resonates with audiences worldwide.

In the following chapters, we will delve deeper into the specifics of investing in private placements within the entertainment and media sector. We will explore the various sub-sectors, such as film production, music labels, and digital media platforms, providing insights into the unique considerations and potential risks and rewards associated with each.

Whether you are interested in financing the next breakout independent film or supporting the development of cutting-edge digital media platforms, investing in entertainment and media private placements offers a thrilling opportunity to be part of the ever-evolving landscape of content creation and consumption.

Evaluating Entertainment and Media Investment Opportunities

Introduction:

In today's digital age, the entertainment and media industry is experiencing a significant transformation. With the advent of new technologies and platforms, investors are presented with a wide range of investment opportunities in this sector. However, evaluating these opportunities requires a comprehensive understanding of the unique dynamics and risks associated with entertainment and media ventures. This subchapter aims to guide investors through the process of evaluating potential investment opportunities in the entertainment and media industry.

Key Factors to Consider:

1. Market Analysis: Before investing in an entertainment or media venture, it is crucial to conduct a thorough market analysis. This involves understanding the target audience, competition, industry trends, and potential growth opportunities. A market analysis will help investors identify potential risks and assess the viability of the investment opportunity.

2. Intellectual Property: Intellectual property plays a pivotal role in the entertainment and media industry. Evaluating the strength and potential value of the intellectual property associated with a project is essential. This includes assessing copyrights, trademarks, patents, and licensing agreements. Investors should also consider the potential for future intellectual property acquisitions or partnerships.

3. Management Team: The success of an entertainment or media venture heavily relies on the expertise and experience of the management team. Investors should evaluate the track record of the team members, their past successes, and their ability to execute the business plan effectively. Additionally, understanding the team's

network and industry connections can provide valuable insights into the venture's potential success.

4. Financial Analysis: Conducting a thorough financial analysis is crucial when evaluating entertainment and media investment opportunities. This includes assessing the revenue model, cost structure, projected cash flows, and profitability. Investors should also consider the potential for ancillary revenue streams, such as licensing, merchandising, and international distribution.

5. Risk Assessment: Investing in the entertainment and media industry inherently carries certain risks. Investors should carefully evaluate the specific risks associated with a particular opportunity, such as market volatility, changing consumer preferences, regulatory challenges, and technological disruptions. Understanding and mitigating these risks is crucial before making any investment decisions.

Conclusion:

Investing in entertainment and media ventures can offer lucrative opportunities for investors. However, it requires a thorough evaluation of market dynamics, intellectual property, management team, financials, and risks. By considering these key factors, investors can make informed decisions and maximize their chances of success in this exciting and ever-evolving industry.

Due Diligence for Entertainment and Media Private Placements

Investing in private placements in the entertainment and media industry can offer exciting opportunities for investors looking to diversify their portfolios and tap into the potential of this dynamic sector. However, it is crucial to conduct thorough due diligence before committing your capital to any venture in this niche.

When investing in entertainment and media private placements, it is essential to consider the following key factors:

1. Industry Expertise: Understand the nuances of the entertainment and media industry. Familiarize yourself with the different segments, such as film, television, music, digital media, and gaming. Gain knowledge about current trends, market size, and the competitive landscape.

2. Management Team: Evaluate the expertise and track record of the management team. Look for individuals with relevant experience in the industry who have demonstrated their ability to execute successful projects. Assess their ability to navigate the ever-evolving media landscape and their understanding of market dynamics.

3. Intellectual Property: Intellectual property rights are crucial in the entertainment and media industry. Evaluate the portfolio of copyrights, trademarks, patents, and licenses held by the company. Assess the potential for revenue generation and the long-term viability of the intellectual property.

4. Revenue Streams: Analyze the company's revenue streams and their potential for growth. Look for diversified revenue sources, such as advertising, subscriptions, licensing, and merchandising. Assess the stability and scalability of these revenue streams to determine the company's financial sustainability.

5. Market Analysis: Conduct a comprehensive market analysis to assess the target audience, market size, and potential for growth. Understand the competitive landscape and identify the unique selling propositions of the company's products or services. Evaluate the market demand and the company's ability to capture a significant market share.

6. Financial Performance: Review the company's financial statements, including revenue, expenses, and profitability. Assess the historical financial performance and projections for the future.

Evaluate the company's ability to generate positive cash flows and its financial stability.

7. Risk Assessment: Identify and evaluate the risks associated with investing in entertainment and media private placements. These may include regulatory risks, market uncertainties, technological disruptions, and changing consumer preferences. Assess the mitigating strategies put in place by the company to manage these risks effectively.

By conducting thorough due diligence in these areas, investors can make informed decisions when investing in entertainment and media private placements. Remember to consult with legal, financial, and industry experts to gain a comprehensive understanding of the opportunities and risks involved. This will help you maximize your chances of success and minimize potential pitfalls in this exciting investment niche.

Investment Strategies for Entertainment and Media Private Placements

In the fast-paced world of entertainment and media, private placements offer unique investment opportunities for individuals looking to capitalize on the industry's growth and potential. This subchapter will delve into the various investment strategies that can be employed when considering private placements in the entertainment and media sector.

1. Research and Due Diligence: Before diving into any investment opportunity, it is crucial to conduct thorough research and due diligence. This includes analyzing the financial health, historical performance, and growth potential of the entertainment or media company seeking private funding. Understanding the market

dynamics, competitive landscape, and industry trends will provide valuable insights to make informed investment decisions.

2. Diversification: Just like any investment portfolio, diversification is key when investing in entertainment and media private placements. By spreading investments across different subsectors such as film production, music labels, streaming services, or gaming companies, investors can mitigate risks and maximize returns. Diversification also allows for exposure to different revenue streams and potential growth areas within the industry.

3. Partnering with Industry Experts: Investing in private placements can be complex, especially in niche sectors like entertainment and media. As such, partnering with industry experts, such as venture capital firms or angel investors, can provide valuable guidance and access to exclusive investment opportunities. These experts possess the necessary industry knowledge and network to identify promising ventures and mitigate risks.

4. Long-term Vision: The entertainment and media industry is known for its volatility and constant evolution. Therefore, investors should adopt a long-term vision and be prepared to hold investments for an extended period. This allows for potential value creation and the ability to weather short-term market fluctuations.

5. Risk Management: As with any investment, risk management should be a priority. Understanding the potential risks associated with entertainment and media private placements, such as changing consumer preferences, technological disruptions, or regulatory challenges, is crucial. Implementing risk mitigation strategies like thorough contract analysis, diversification, and ongoing monitoring can help protect investments.

6. Staying Informed: The entertainment and media landscape is constantly evolving. Therefore, investors must stay informed about emerging trends, regulatory changes, and industry dynamics. This

can be achieved by attending industry conferences, following industry publications, and engaging with professionals in the field. Investing in entertainment and media private placements can be both exciting and rewarding. By employing these investment strategies, investors can navigate the unique challenges and opportunities in the industry, ultimately maximizing their returns while supporting the growth of this vibrant sector.

Chapter 12: Conclusion

Recap of Private Placements Investing Strategies

In this subchapter, we will recap some of the key strategies for investing in private placements. Private placements offer investors exclusive opportunities to invest in various sectors such as real estate, startups, biotech companies, renewable energy projects, art and collectibles, technology companies, healthcare startups, food and beverage businesses, social impact projects, and entertainment and media ventures. Understanding the strategies behind successful private placements investing can help you make informed decisions and maximize your returns.

1. Diversification: One of the most important strategies when investing in private placements is to diversify your portfolio. By spreading your investments across different sectors, you reduce the risk associated with any one investment. This way, even if one sector

underperforms, your other investments can potentially balance out the losses.

2. Thorough Due Diligence: Before investing in any private placement opportunity, it is crucial to conduct thorough due diligence. Research the company or project extensively, assessing its financial health, management team, market potential, and competitive landscape. Engage with industry experts, review financial statements, and evaluate the risks involved. Only invest if you are confident in the viability and potential of the opportunity.

3. Understand your Risk Tolerance: Private placements can be high-risk investments, as they often involve early-stage companies or projects. It is important to assess your risk tolerance and invest accordingly. Consider your financial goals, investment horizon, and the potential impact of any losses. If you have a lower risk tolerance, focus on more established sectors or companies within private placements.

4. Seek Professional Advice: Investing in private placements can be complex, especially in specific niches such as biotech companies or renewable energy projects. It is advisable to seek professional advice from experienced financial advisors or investment professionals who specialize in these areas. They can provide valuable insights, mitigate risks, and help you navigate the intricacies of private placements investing.

5. Stay Informed: The private placements market is constantly evolving, and new opportunities arise regularly. Stay informed about the latest trends, regulations, and emerging sectors within the private placements landscape. Subscribe to industry publications, attend conferences, and network with other investors to gain access to exclusive opportunities.

By following these strategies, you can enhance your private placements investing approach and increase your chances of success. Remember, private placements offer unique investment possibilities, but they require thorough research, careful assessment of risks, and a diversified portfolio to optimize your returns.

Final Thoughts and Recommendations for Investors

Congratulations! By reading this book, you have taken the first step towards understanding the world of private placements and unlocking exclusive investment opportunities. Before we conclude, we would like to leave you with some final thoughts and recommendations to guide you on your journey as an investor.

1. Diversify Your Portfolio: As an investor, it is essential to diversify your portfolio across different asset classes, industries, and geographical regions. Private placements offer a unique opportunity to invest in a wide range of niches, from real estate and startups to biotech companies and renewable energy projects. By diversifying your investments, you can minimize risks and maximize potential returns.

2. Conduct Thorough Due Diligence: Before investing in any private placement, it is crucial to conduct thorough due diligence. This includes researching the company or project, evaluating the management team, analyzing the financials, and understanding the market dynamics. Seek professional advice if needed and never invest in something you do not fully understand.

3. Understand the Risks: Private placements come with inherent risks, and it is important to be aware of them. These risks can include illiquidity, lack of transparency, regulatory challenges, and the potential for loss of capital. While the potential rewards can be significant, it is essential to assess your risk appetite and invest accordingly.

4. Leverage Expertise and Networks: Investing in private placements often requires specialized knowledge and connections. Consider partnering with professionals, such as investment advisors, brokers, or crowdfunding platforms, who have experience in the specific niche you are interested in. They can provide valuable insights, access to exclusive opportunities, and help navigate the complexities of the investment process.

5. Align with Your Values: Private placements offer the unique advantage of investing in projects and companies that align with your values and passions. Whether it is supporting social impact projects, renewable energy initiatives, or art and collectibles, consider investing in projects that resonate with your personal beliefs. Not only will this increase your satisfaction as an investor, but it can also contribute to positive social change.

In conclusion, investing in private placements can be a rewarding and lucrative endeavor for investors. By diversifying your portfolio, conducting thorough due diligence, understanding the risks, leveraging expertise, and aligning with your values, you can make informed investment decisions and unlock exclusive opportunities in various niches. Remember, knowledge is power, so continue to educate yourself, stay updated on market trends, and seize the opportunities that private placements offer. Good luck on your investment journey!

Appendices: Venture Exchanges

Venture Stock Exchanges in the World

1. New York Stock Exchange (NYSE) - United States
2. NASDAQ - United States
3. London Stock Exchange (LSE) - United Kingdom
4. Tokyo Stock Exchange (TSE) - Japan
5. Shanghai Stock Exchange (SSE) - China
6.
7. Hong Kong Stock Exchange (HKEX) - Hong Kong
8.
9. Euronext - European Union
10.
11. Toronto Stock Exchange (TSX) - Canada
12. Bombay Stock Exchange (BSE) - India
13. Australian Securities Exchange (ASX) - Australia
14.
15. Korea Exchange (KRX) - South Korea
16. Deutsche Börse - Germany
17. Johannesburg Stock Exchange (JSE) - South Africa
18. B3 (Brazil, Bolsa, Balcão) - Brazil
19. Moscow Exchange (MOEX) - Russia

20.
21. Singapore Exchange (SGX) - Singapore
22. Taiwan Stock Exchange (TWSE) - Taiwan
23.
24. Madrid Stock Exchange (BME) - Spain
25. Mexican Stock Exchange (BMV) - Mexico
26. Istanbul Stock Exchange (BIST) - Turkey

Please note that this list is not exhaustive, and there are other regional and local stock exchanges around the world that may also facilitate venture stock trading.

How to Participate in the Toronto Venture Exchange

1. Understand the TSXV: Familiarize yourself with the TSXV's purpose, structure, and requirements. It is a stock exchange

focused on early-stage and emerging companies, providing a platform for these companies to raise capital and grow.

2. Meet the listing requirements: Ensure that your company meets the listing requirements set by the TSXV. These requirements include financial thresholds, minimum number of shareholders, and a certain level of working capital. Consult the TSXV's website or contact their listing department for detailed information.

3. Engage a qualified advisor: Seek guidance from a qualified advisor, such as a lawyer or an investment bank, who has experience with TSXV listings. They can assist you in navigating the listing process and provide expertise on compliance and regulatory matters.

4. Prepare the necessary documents: Prepare the required documents for submission, including financial statements, business plan, prospectus, and legal opinions. These documents must comply with the TSXV's guidelines and standards.

5. Submit the application: Submit your application to the TSXV along with all the required documents. The TSXV will review your application and may request additional information or clarification.

6. Complete due diligence: Undergo a due diligence process, where the TSXV will review your company's financial, legal, and operational aspects. This process ensures that your company meets the exchange's standards and requirements.

1. Obtain necessary approvals: Obtain any necessary approvals, such as shareholder approvals or regulatory clearances, as required by the TSXV.

2. Pay the listing fees: Pay the applicable fees, which include an initial listing fee and annual listing fees, as determined by the TSXV.

3. Listing and trading: Upon successful completion of the listing process and meeting all requirements, your company

will be listed on the TSXV. Your company's shares will be available for trading on the exchange.

4. Comply with ongoing obligations: Once listed, your company must comply with the TSXV's ongoing obligations, including financial reporting requirements, disclosure obligations, and corporate governance standards.

It is important to note that the TSXV listing process can be complex and time-consuming. Seeking professional advice and assistance is highly recommended to ensure a smooth and successful listing experience.

Where to find Private Placement Investment Opportunities

Private placement investments are typically not publicly advertised or listed on traditional investment platforms. Instead, they are typically offered through private networks, broker-dealers, investment banks, or other financial institutions. Here are a few places where you can find private placement investment listings:

1. Private Placement Memorandum (PPM): A PPM is a legal document that outlines the terms and conditions of a private placement investment. Companies looking to raise capital through private placements often distribute PPMs to potential investors. You can search for PPMs online or contact investment banks or broker-dealers to inquire about available offerings.
2. Accredited Investor Networks: There are various networks and online platforms that connect accredited investors with private placement investment opportunities. Some popular examples include AngelList, SeedInvest, and CircleUp. These platforms often require investors to meet certain income or net worth thresholds to participate.
3. Investment Banks and Broker-Dealers: Investment banks and broker-dealers often have access to private placement investment opportunities. They have relationships with companies seeking capital and can provide information about available placements to their clients. Contact local investment banks or broker-dealers to inquire about private placement opportunities.
4. Wealth Management Firms: Some wealth management firms specialize in offering private placement investments to their high-net-worth clients. If you work with a wealth management firm, reach out to your advisor or contact other firms specializing in alternative investments to inquire about available offerings.

1. Industry Associations and Networking Events: Attending industry conferences, seminars, or networking events related to the sector you're interested in can provide opportunities to connect with companies and individuals offering private placement investments. These events often

attract high-net-worth individuals, venture capitalists, and companies seeking capital.

Remember, private placements are typically restricted to accredited investors who meet specific income or net worth requirements. It's important to do thorough due diligence and consult with a financial advisor before investing in any private placement opportunity.

PrivatePlacements.com is one of the best places I have found that has a very extensive list of Private Placement investment opportunities. PrivatePlacements.com is the only platform that aggregates, analyzes, and delivers daily, free information about private placements activity in the Canadian public capital markets. We gather and report private placements data from every Canadian exchange and company, empowering investors to stay abreast of the financing landscape without wasting hours digging through granular public data.

It is the perfect tool for Investors, Analysts, Management Teams, Traders, Service Providers.

1. Obsessive focus on investor experience, optimized for mobile and desktop
2. Comprehensive analysis of all brokered and non-brokered Canadian private placements
3. Daily updates—bookmark and track where capital is flowing
4. In-depth term sheets that list price, total proceeds, number of shares, warrants, lead agent, financing type, and more
5. Warrants expiry calendar with upcoming exercise dates and strike prices
6. Interactive financing tables sortable by date, sector, company, price, and agent
7. Daily articles and routine deep dives into company and industry catalysts

Made in United States
Troutdale, OR
12/29/2023

16539288R00056